The

LADIES
LIVING
Guide

Keeping *IT* together from A-Z

KARA Y. WELLS

with Relationship Expert GEORGE JAMES, LMFT

The Ladies Living Guide: Keeping IT Together From A-Z
ISBN-13: 978-0692334027
ISBN-10: 0692334025

Book Design: SharonBrewsterDesign.com
Kara Wells' Photo: Joanna Petit-Frere, Visage One Studios
Fashion: Kristyn of BEvolution
Makeup: Joanna Petit-Frere
George James photo and biography courtesy of GeorgeTalks.com

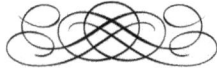

DEDICATION

Mom
WILBERANNE DREHER WELLS
IT all started with you

The
LADIES
LIVING
Guide

Keeping *IT* together from A-Z

CONTENTS

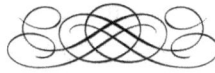

PROLOGUE

The Ladies Living Guide is a compilation of thoughts about women and how we handle emotion. It is designed to provoke thought, prevent pessimism and produce healthy relationships.

The LLG also helps one learn how to:
- **Relate and communicate**
- **Embrace the feelings that affect emotion**
- **Navigate and categorize feelings properly**

Developing these abilities helps a woman move from womanhood to 'ladyhood.' A true lady is defined by her ability to maintain grace under pressure, and this guide will offer strategies on how to do just that.

One of the keys to 'ladyhood' is emotional stability. Emotional stability, or peace of mind, seems so far away for so many. Sometimes as women, we tend to react off of emotion instead of logic and often let our emotions affect our ability to communicate effectively. Contrary to our popular belief, men tend to be more logical than emotional. They process better under pressure and tend to make sense out of seemingly senseless situations. Therefore, it was necessary to ask a male to co-author *The Ladies Living Guide*. It is impossible for me to be a woman and also interpret what it is like to be a woman without bias, so thank God for George!

George James is the founder and CEO of George Talks, LLC. *George Talks* around the world about building and maintaining healthy relationships. In the LLG he will *talk* to us and give us sound advice on how to be emotionally mature and make positive life choices.

The Ladies' Living Guide is a quick reference guide, giving practical advice on how to stay in control of your emotion. Simply put, it will put you on a path to emotional wellness and subsequently learn how to keep *IT* together.

The LLG will also help you foster healthy relationships, keep your peace of mind, and help you live in the freedom of being a lady.

We hope this book positively impacts your life and restores and redefines the LADY in you!

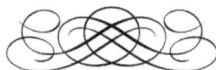

– THOUGHT ONE –
PEACE OF MIND AND THE *IT* DEFINED

Is having peace of mind really possible? Is there a way to control your actions while monitoring your reactions? The answer is yes. Peace of mind is possible, but in order to obtain peace, you must first learn how to operate in it. Having peace of mind is the foundation for healthy living. Most people cannot function well in chaos and need harmony in their lives. Being able to maintain peace in your mind is the result of monitoring and maintaining one's *IT*.

There was, and will always be, an *IT* we have to keep together. But what is this *IT*? I would like to think of it as an abbreviation for Internal Transmitter. An internal transmitter is an invisible gauge or signal that operates daily, controlling and monitoring your actions and reactions.

Here's the break down.

The I stands for internal. Internal pertains to anything on the inside: the inner part of one's being. The T stands for transmitter. A transmitter is any person or object that transmits.

To transmit means:
• To convey, communicate
• To pass on or spread

Read the definitions again. When trying to determine how you are communicating, you first have to know what's on the inside. "Out of the abundance of the heart, the mouth speaks." What you hear internally will be heard externally when you are not in control of your emotion. Once you are emotionally stable you can transmit, convey and communicate effectively so that everyone understands what is truly on your heart.

Your *IT* is yours, and far too often, other people come into your life and alter or change it. Your *IT* determines your level of sanity and security. What occurs emotionally and internally will always affect your *IT* therefore it has to be monitored and controlled on a continuous basis.

The I is important because from the "inside" stems a root cause to every action and reaction. Sometimes what has been carelessly transmitted to us gets carelessly transmitted to others. Something in our past influences our current decision-making and filtering process, which makes us vulnerable. When we feel weak or inadequate, we tend to overcompensate for the shortcomings. Every individual shows this weakness differently, but it shows up in all of us at some point. This is the reason why, in some situations, we find it harder to keep our *IT* together than others. Later in the text when emotion is defined, you will find a list of emotionally weak characteristics. These are signature habits of individuals covering up internal weaknesses.

It is okay for you to read the list and find yourself on it. We all have been there before and constantly work at staying off. The goal is for you to accept and admit the weakness; that's the road to strength.

This guide will convert the fragile emotions into strong ones. You were made special with characteristics unique to you. Learn how to embrace them and see what happens when the weak become empowered. You will have peace of mind by knowing how to keep *IT* together.

Disclaimer: This guide is not the answer to all of life's woes, but please don't take it lightly either. The LLG is designed to help you LIVE life to the fullest! No longer blaming anyone else; learn how to admit shortcomings and monitor and adjust your behavior so that you and your surroundings stay at stable.

In order to maintain your *IT*, you must know how your *IT* has been affected by the 3 E's.

The 3 E's are environment, experience, and exposure. *You are what you eat*; a product of your environment, a collection of your experiences and limited by your exposure.

Don't allow a negative environment, a negative experience and negative exposure to affect your *IT*. Take the time to explore the positives. Eat off what you need to live well and discipline yourself to take in environments, experiences and exposures necessary for the results you want.

George and I are your emotional strength trainers. From A–Z, we uncover words and From A–Z, we uncover words and explore their function and purpose in your life. You must first identify the issue before you can do anything about it. We've done that part for you. We identify the issues and then give advice and suggestions to live a healthier life. The real work is up to you!

Allow this guide to create a space for personal internal reflection as well as corporate and transparent progression. With this guide, a lady's life will be a lot easier to live!

– THOUGHT TWO –
WOMAN VS. LADY

Growing up I often heard the phrase "every lady is a woman, but not every woman is a lady" and wondered if it was true. How can something be everything and nothing all at the same time? How could a lady be a woman, but a woman not be a lady? Is this possible?

The answer is YES! Yes, it is possible for a lady to be a woman but a woman not be a lady, look at how the words are defined.

According to Merriam-Webster's dictionary, a woman is defined as an adult female person or an adult female human belonging to a specific gender; Womankind.

The definition of a woman is non-descriptive and gives no attributes to being a woman other than being born. This means every female born to the human race is designed to grow into a woman, distinctively feminine in nature.

The definition of a lady however is very descriptive. It assumes the reader understands that a lady is a woman first and then adds the qualities and characteristics that define her.

The American Heritage Dictionary defines lady as a woman of high social standing or refinement, especially when viewed as dignified and well-mannered; a woman who is the head of a household.

After reading and understanding the difference between a woman and a lady, I deduced that there are a lot of women in the world but not so many ladies. Where are the women who walk with refinement and dignity while maintaining a developed demeanor? There are a lot of single mothers, but how many do we see functioning in the role of a lady; running well-mannered households? These questions left me determined to redefine how the world views a lady and how we view ourselves.

In my opinion, First Ladies Jacqueline Kennedy and Michelle Obama, represent the epitome of 'ladyhood.' Every day Lady Michelle subconsciously works to restore the image of what a true lady is. A true lady is elegant and educated, cultured and classy, dignified and determined.

A well-mannered woman is a lady. In order to walk in grace and refinement, you must be able to understand, interpret, and analyze any situation before you react to it.

Activating your *IT* (internal transmitter) is the beginning of embracing 'ladyhood.' In today's society where so many single women are the head of a household, in order to maintain your home you must maintain your IT. A disturbed and disrupted transmitter can affect everything around you. This Ladies Living Guide will give you strategies and help you uncover the issues that may be prohibiting the lady in you from being revealed.

Becoming more than a woman, becoming a lady, takes work. Don't be afraid to face the fears or issues that may be deeply rooted that cause you to not walk in 'ladyhood.' I've heard that hurt people, hurt people. With the LLG you can learn how to monitor and adjust your reactions so that even if you are hurt, you won't hurt anyone else.

Use the guide as an opportunity to reflect on your past, repair your present, and release yourself for your future! Learn how to not just be a woman, but become a lady!

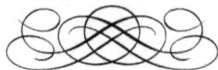

– THOUGHT THREE –
EMOTIONS: WHAT ARE THEY?

Emotions: What are they?

♪♪It's just emotion taking me over Caught up in sorrow Lost in the song ♪

EMOTIONS – They take us over. We get lost in them. They can be overwhelming and take us to extremes on either side of the coin. They are polar opposites in need of balance. Feelings of joy can easily turn to sadness, love to hate, happiness to anger, and generosity to greed. But are emotions even real? Do they even exist? Do feelings have authority over thought process and decision making?

If you learned that emotions and feelings are the same then your answer would be yes; feelings do have authority over my thought process and decision making. What you learned was only part true; feelings are real but they really have no authority. The only authority they have is what you give them. There are many feelings but only one emotion. Your emotion is your mental state of being that gets affected by your feelings. The real definition of emotion has little to do with what you feel, but everything to do with what you know about what you feel.

The American Heritage Dictionary defines emotion as a mental state that arises spontaneously rather than through conscious effort and is often accompanied by physiological changes.

In other words, the condition or state of your mind changes based your natural internal impulses rather than by a conscious effort to do what is right. To be emotional is to not be aware or attentive to the fullness of the matter at hand, and this reaction many times causes outward or physical differences.

Every individual has one mind. That one mind has a state of being. Either it "is" or it "is not." Consequently, emotional stability can determine one's mental state and that state can be classified as being weak or strong. Is your mind emotionally strong or emotionally weak? Can you be fully aware of and assess a situation without being spontaneous in your reaction all of the time?

If you confidently answered yes, then you may not need this living guide. But if you answered NO or are unsure, KEEP READING!

What is emotional weakness? How do I determine if I am emotionally weak or strong, and what do I do about it?

Here are some practical steps:

1. *Learn yourself* — Identify how you display evidence of emotional weakness.

Below we've listed some signs and characteristics.

Signs and Characteristics of being Emotionally Weak

aggressive	opinions	late	rarely laughs aloud
abusive	forgetful	lazy	reluctant to lead
acts as a martyr	gloomy	life spectator	restless
appears phony	hard to get	likes to suffer	sarcastic
analytical	along with	makes excuses	seeks approval
cries easily	hesitant to	makes fun of others	selfish
critical of others and	start anything	moody	self-righteous
any imperfections	holds grudges	naïve	stingy
depressive	hypochondriac	no conviction	suspicious of others
discouraging	humiliating	not cordial	stubborn
dislikes	impractical	opposes change	talks a lot
opposition	impulsive	overprotective of self	teases
disorganized	inattentive	overbearing	theoretical
dominating	inconsiderate	passive	unenthusiastic
easily distracted	inconsistent	pessimistic	uses people
easily hurt by others	indecisive	perfectionist	undependable
emotionally	indifferent	picky	undisciplined
unpredictable	judgmental	prolongs animosity	ungrateful
erupts into anger	lacks motivation	procrastinates	weak-willed
exaggerates	lacks self-confidence	proud	worries a lot
fearful of others'	lacks self-control	quick tongued	

See anything you recognize? Either consciously or subconsciously both men and women alike tend to display some of these characteristics to mask or hide what they are really feeling. Communicating how you feel can help you identify the actions and reactions thus allowing you the chance to control and monitor them.

2. *Accept and love yourself* — Once you've identified your weak areas, you will have to accept them and move on. To accept emotional weakness is no more than accepting the fact that you are human and you need healthy relationships with others.

Mixed-up and misguided feelings often alter your state of mind and leave you emotionally weak and vulnerable. Reflect on and recognize what might have happened to you that made you weak. You may uncover an answer, or you may not, but once you accept weakness, the road to emotional strength gets paved with your *willingness* to be mentally strong and emotionally stable.

3. *Reveal yourself* — Do not be afraid! Once you have accepted your weaknesses, reveal them to someone you trust who may be different from you. If you are not motivated, start hanging with people who are. Revealing your weakness to a trusted friend, mentor, or spiritual leader is a sign of acceptance, accountability, and maturity. It may take some time to get to this point, but it makes for healthy, successful relationships.

One's ability to be emotionally stable is a contributing factor in determining the difference between being a woman and being a lady. This book addresses potential LADIES – women determined to be more than "human adult females" with feelings.

The LLG will restore the image of what it means to be "a lady:" elegant and educated, cultured and classy, dignified and determined. Being a lady sets a standard. You will raise your expectations and outlook of yourself and positively affect those around you. With high expectations the sky is the limit and you'll no longer be driven by others but motivated by the love you have for yourself.

Remember to identify your weaknesses so you can accept yourself, love yourself and reveal yourself to others. We know that changing your perspective is not easy but don't be afraid to *"be transformed by the renewing of your mind."* Take from the guide what you need to build healthy and prosperous relationships and give life a chance no matter what you have been through.

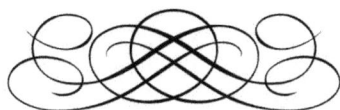

THE GUIDE
A–Z

"The LLG will restore the image
of what it means to be a lady."

THE GUIDE
A–Z

Adjust
Behavior
Control
Demonstrate
Emotion
Forgive
Goodness
Humility
Identity

Just
Kindle
Listen
Manners
Navigate
Opinion
Patience
Question
Reaction

Satisfied
Ten
Understanding
Volume
Wisdom
Xerxes
Yourself
Zealous

A

AD · JUST

to change (something) so that it fits, corresponds, or conforms; adapt; accommodate; to settle or bring to a satisfactory state, so that parties are agreed in the result.

Issue: Our perspective, attitude, approach, and responses need to be flexible and open to receive. Sometimes they need to fit, correspond, or conform. We may have to adjust in order to settle or bring something to a satisfactory state.

Ladies, how often do we do this? We either do it too much or not enough. Adjusting for us is not a simple task, but we constantly feel others should do it for us. In our emotionally weak state we demand what we want, when, why, where, and how we want it. Does this paint a fair and healthy picture? *(See J)*

Most of the time, because of how we feel, we don't want to adjust what we feel. Somehow we've made up in our minds that our feelings are justified, and sometimes they are, but check your internal transmitter. Are you keeping *IT* together as you form your reactions?

Feelings generally determine your attitude. Attitude is the one thing we all have but tend to deny. It is a key factor in adjusting. We must be able to pinpoint when our attitude(s) need adjusting and do it!

Pinpointing the need for attitude adjustment is a process that you must be *willing* to undertake. Along with willingness, it takes other skills to follow the process through. These skills include *awareness, acceptance, and admission (See I)*. Following these steps will increase your emotional strength. So instead of holding a grudge or carrying an attitude you can let it go and receive. Understanding how these A's work in harmony will help you keep *IT* together.

Awareness – Be alert and vigilant at all times. In order to be aware of how people and situations are affecting you, you must first know who you are. *(See I)* Knowing who you are tends to predict how you are going to react. Be aware of your emotional weakness.

Acceptance – Accept who you are and how you feel. 98% of the time it is ok to feel how you feel; it's just not ok to make others suffer for it. Acceptance is a great counterpart to forgiveness. It suggests that you identify and accept your role in the situation, which will lead you to forgiving the other person and accepting them for their shortcomings as well. *(See F)*

Admission – Admit your feelings if you can. Share with the other party how you are feeling, no matter where it leads you; at least then you will have let the other person know how they have affected you. When sharing how you feel remember to watch your volume! *(See V)*

Adjustment – Adhering to the above will cause an automatic adjustment in attitude. It's not easy but it will make room for clarity and compromise. Not giving in to your emotional weakness and adjusting your attitude will help you keep *IT* together.

GEORGE TALKS…

Adjusting can be difficult for many people. It can feel like you are giving something up. In addition, if you feel like you've given up a lot in your relationship, most people try to stand their ground even more each time an opportunity comes up to adjust. When you don't adjust and you say or do whatever you want to, people tend to stop talking to you, interacting with you, or developing quality relationships with you.

Take the chance; make the adjustment, and you will see the benefits. When women are able to share their perspective and make adjustments, men believe they can work with you and are willing to adjust themselves.

B

BE·HAV·IOR

manner of behaving or acting; observable activity in a human or animal.

Issue: Our behavior tends to be more spontaneous and animalistic than it should be. It is difficult to act in a manner befitting a lady at all times.

Ladies, where does bad behavior come from? Negative reactions to the simplest of circumstances, has a root cause. There is a reason why we behave the way we do. 99.9% of the time we react the way we do because of our collection of negative experiences in the area of relationship (all kinds). As a result our mind stays in bondage or captivity to these experiences, resulting in negative, pessimistic reactions. *(See R)*

How emotional bondage affects you is tricky because you can't see it. It unassumingly influences your behavior by keeping your heart and mind wrapped in negativity, torment and pain. As a result the negativity has no choice but to spill over into the relationships we try to have. Have you ever met a person who complained all the time? If so, they may be in the bondage that affects behavior. They may not be free to live everyday expecting greatness but merely exist to let life happen to them instead of living life to its fullest potential. The most you can do for those constant complainers is buy them this book and move on; remember that *"misery loves company!"*

Different past experiences, breed different results. Sometimes negative past experiences affect current behaviors. From complaining to promiscuity – do not stay in bondage to past hurts! Don't let your past have a negative effect on your present behaviors. Learn how to behave, be what others aspire to be by having observable manners, which reflect dignity, respect for self, love, and, most of all, emotional stability! Enter every relationship, conversation, and situation open to what the universe wants to bring you, and remember, what you put out is what you get back! Release the bondage and keep *IT* together.

GEORGE TALKS...

Do you think behavior is contagious? Well, it is!
The good you do inspires, challenges, and motivates others to behave that way. The same happens with negative behavior. What do you want your children, family members, or partner to learn from your behavior? Changing your behavior means being intentional. It means everything you feel you want to do, you can't do.

What is the end result you want to produce? Once you figure that out, then you ask yourself, what I need to do or say to get that result. Women who are able to do this come off as caring and confident versus irrational and juvenile.

C

CON · TROL

to exercise restraint or direction over; dominate; command

Issue: We are so used to being in charge, we want control over everything and everyone but we won't admit it.

Control! Control! Control!

Ladies, Guess what? We don't have to have it!

I know, I know; we've been running things for so long that it just comes naturally. We're CEO's, teachers, community leaders, businesses owners and mothers. We tell people what to do all the time. We are, most of the time, ALWAYS in control of someone or something. But do we have to control everything or everyone around us? Must we really dominate all the conversations with our opinions *(see O)*, or always want things to go our way, just because, and at any cost? This behavior, for some mild, others extreme, is YOU desiring full control. Not being willing to relinquish it will only help you NOT keep *IT* together when things get rough.

The funny thing is that a lot of us try to take control over things we have no control over, like other people! How did we become such dictators? People (especially our men) are human (spirit) beings who have feelings that they want to have respected, too. When we don't relinquish control, we don't honor those feelings. As a result we lose that relationship, job, or program because we gripped it so tightly we crushed or killed it.

Letting go of control is paying honor, homage and respect to all parties while allowing you to be an active participant in the conversation or situation. *(See L)*

Let's learn how to monitor and properly adjust our controlling behaviors. There's a necessary element of self-control that is needed to keep *IT* together.

GEORGE TALKS...

Who can we really control? Honestly, we have the most control over ourselves. People frustrate us, disappoint us, and hurt us. Often times to avoid these feelings, we try to control other people and situations. But it forces us to still experience the very thing we are trying to avoid. The more you try to exert your power over someone else, the more they will push back and rebel.

There is a reason why we have a saying "you catch more bees with honey than vinegar." Using control is like using vinegar. You get the opposite result. Most men detest the feeling of being controlled and will do whatever they can (consciously and unconsciously, fair and unfair) to fight against that control. That could be not committing, being vague, or even cheating. On the other side, you shouldn't be controlled or feel the only way to be with someone is to give up all or most of your rights.

D

DEM · ON · STRATE

to explain, or illustrate by examples, to manifest or exhibit; show

Issue: We are not demonstrating or exhibiting appropriate behaviors.

Ladies demonstrate! Go ahead — walk the runway and MODEL! Be the example of the behavior you want to see. The acts of demonstrating positive behaviors can be connected to that old saying "treat others the way you want to be treated."

Imagine that every time you spoke or engaged in conversation, that someone was holding up a mirror. In that mirror, on public display, was your reflection. What would your reflection show? What behaviors are you demonstrating?

With little eyes looking up at us, the next generation needs to see women of femininity and virtue, honor, and integrity as their examples. In order to save the future we must preserve the present, and that begins with you!

Each lady living is a divine demonstration of goodness, grace, and glory that should be cherished and put on a pedestal. Modeling goodness looks like the state of being good *(See G)*. Exemplifying grace has two purposes; being controlled and polite and demonstrating diving favor from God. Both of which, extend compassion and empathy for others.

Modeling appropriate behavior takes work you can keep *IT* together by being the example you want to see.

GEORGE TALKS...

As much as we say we will be different than our mothers and fathers, as much as we say we will not repeat the same destructive patterns, we still end up being like them. Demonstrating also means changing the cycle; just because your parent cursed at you or didn't show up for you or was mean to you doesn't mean you have to do the same thing.

You have the power to demonstrate new and better behavior. Be the person you have always wanted to be. Demonstrate a new you, and you will change generations to come.

E

E·MO·TION(S)

a state of mind or any strong agitation of the feelings aroused by experiencing love, hate, fear, etc., and usually accompanied by certain physiological changes, as increased heartbeat or respiration, and often overt manifestation, as crying or shaking.

Issue: We are emotionally fragile and have limited control of how our feelings make us react.

E-M-O-T-I-O-N-S—Ladies, we must learn to CONTROL them! In order to do that we must first know what they are, where they come from, and how they work. Then you can use this guide as a framework to manage your feelings and put you on a path to emotional wellness.

Emotions in simplest terms are feelings or expressions of feeling that can be positive or negative. Our pride generally dictates how we react to something/someone, based on how we feel about what they are saying and how they are saying it. *(See H)*

In order to keep *IT* together we must be willing to compartmentalize our emotions and use the right ones for the right reasons. Emotions are wonderful blessings that, when handled properly, will make life worth living. Your feelings are important and should be valued, but they should not lead, guide, or make decisions for you. Emotions tend to get ignited when pride gets affected. It's a natural reaction. In order to organize our emotions we must put our pride aside. *"But I'm not prideful ..."* *"I don't think highly or myself ..."* Well, I'm sorry to say, if you don't think you're prideful, that's pride.

We all allow a little pride and ego to get in the way sometimes. Just ask yourself, have you ever wanted to have your way? When that happens; what do you do? You let your emotions get the best of you, take over the conversation, and say something that will get a reaction out of the other person. This tends to happen when you have a lot of mixed-up feelings and emotions, and your pride wanted to protect them. It's okay; it's natural.

In order to manage your emotions you should first release your pride. It is a shield of defense, a barrier that must come down in order to communicate. Bringing it down, however, will expose your true will and intentions, so get ready! It will always go well if you love yourself and respect how you feel, accept your responsibility/role in the situation, put emotions) in their proper category, and then react.

Ladies, if you learn this, then you will KNOW how to keep IT together.

GEORGE TALKS...

We all have emotions and use our emotions, sometimes in inappropriate ways. The question is how many emotions you have access to and how many emotions do you express to others. When I work with people, one of the things they struggle with is having access to more emotions. Many of us know anger, might admit to sadness, and occasionally happiness. There are more emotions, feelings than the three I just mentioned.

For example there's confusion, excitement, and frustration. When you express yourself, is anger the main emotion you express? You will get more out of life and out of your relationships if you express other emotions. For some, it might mean being vulnerable and showing your softer side, for others it might mean showing frustration instead of rage.

There is more to you than just one or two emotions. Let the world see the complete you. Express yourself!

F

FOR · GIVE

to grant pardon for or remission of (an offense, debt, etc.);
absolve; to cease to feel resentment against

Issue: We either don't completely absolve our problems with people or we don't forget and still resent how someone wronged us and that keeps us from moving forward and having healthy relationships.

Ladies, forgiveness is essential to any successful undertaking, whether it is a marriage, a friendship or a business venture because PEOPLE MAKE MISTAKES. In order to keep *IT* together one must understand the entirety of the situation before reacting out of emotion.

To grant someone a pardon for their actions after they have hurt you is nearly an insurmountable task. It is one that may require distance, patience, and perseverance because you never know how many times you'll have to forgive. If you are willing to let go of the hurt, then you are willing to move on. You must accept and be okay with the fact that majority of people act out of familiarity. When you engage with them (on whatever level), they may not say what you want to hear, when, and how you want to hear it. They may not do what you want, when, and how you want it done, and you must be willing to forgive them for it.

Those of us that live under grace constantly, work at understanding and walking in forgiveness because we are forgiven daily and commanded to walk in love, compassion, grace, and mercy, all equivalents to forgiveness. How can we expect someone to forgive us if we don't forgive? Understanding that it is necessary to forgive, reflect and learn lessons will help us keep *IT* together.

GEORGE TALKS…

Unforgiveness and resentment operate like undetected cancer. It starts small and in one specific area. If it goes unchecked and untreated it begins to grow and then spread throughout the entire body. What started out in the lung or breast is now in the brain, stomach and the entire body.

Many people believe they forgive but when tested, they realize their resentment grew and spread to other areas of their life. For example, you said you forgave him, but years later, you still check his cell phone bill and emails, or you said you forgave your mother, but years later you still won't go visit her and bring your children around unless forced by a death or holiday. Forgiveness is a process and takes time, but when you really do it, you make yourself better and your relationships better.

G

GOOD · NESS

the state or quality of being good, moral excellence;
virtue; strength.

Issue: Being good is not cool. Society tells us it's to be better to be "bad" and as a result we have lost the desire to be and do good to ourselves and others.

Ladies, goodness is the state of being GOOD; which means we are supposed to be good, all of the time. I know you're saying yeah right, who can be good all the time? Don't ask me; I haven't met that person yet. What I do believe is that even though it's difficult to be good all the time, understanding what goodness is will help you stay good, most of the time.

Being good is somewhat equivalent to choosing right or righteousness. You don't have to be perfect, but you should strive to make all of your decisions out of a good, right conscience; not out of emotional instability. Negative emotions tend to affect your ability to be good. Most of us display goodness conditionally: how good others are to you determines how good you are to others. Conditions can't dictate goodness.

You can maintain your state of goodness by maintaining controlled emotions. For example, when you are frustrated, broken, or discouraged, you may be more vulnerable, open, and willing to do things you haven't done or hadn't done in a long time because you are emotionally imbalanced; which could affect goodness.

How do you do it? How do you keep virtue when you're feeling lonely, sad, afraid, hurt, and so on? One suggestion is to seek things that are good: good people, good food, and a source of faith or inspiration. Also, adhere to all the other recommendations in *The Ladies' Living Guide*, which will help you live a good life and keep *IT* together.

GEORGE TALKS...

Being good brings out the good in others. The opposite is true as well. We get into arguments and fights because one person has an attitude that makes the other person raise his or her voice, leading to insults and then a full-blown argument. On the other hand, "I got you something because I was thinking about you," makes the person say, "I'll cook tonight," and it keeps going.

Being good encourages good in others. Being good sets an example for those who watch you, such as children, friends, and romantic partner. Being good produces more positive results than any other option. Give it a try for at least a week nonstop, and you will see the change in others.

H

HU · MIL · I · TY

the quality or condition of being humble; modest opinion or estimate of one's own importance, rank, etc.

Issue: We want to be right all of the time. Humility means putting someone else's idea and opinion above yours.

Now, Ladies, we all know that humility is a taboo word in our "dog eat dog" society. This word causes women to fear that humility (being meek, lowly and submissive) is equivalent to being weak. It most definitely is not! Walking in humility actually puts you at position of strength and authority.

To walk in humility simply means you consider others before yourself, you let go of pride, and are now considering and honoring all involved parties, including yourself. Humility allows you the opportunity to gather, interpret, and report data from the loving, nurturing, guiding perspective. A woman is designed to operate from this place. Doing this will demonstrate how you keep *IT* together.

GEORGE TALKS…

"He or she who is without sin cast the first stone." This quote from The Bible has many references; one of which refers to humility. If we can acknowledge that we all have done wrong at one point or another or that we all have things we are not proud of, then we realize that we are more alike than different. We are not better than each other. Being humble means you realize that you are not better than me, and I am not better than you, so neither of us can cast the stone.

Therefore, we should learn from each other, ask each other for help, be there for each other, and daily practice humility, which is the art of not thinking too highly of yourself while putting others beneath you. This is the art of accepting yourself and others as equals.

I

I · DEN · TI · FY

to recognize or establish as being a particular person or thing;

Issue: Most of us haven't identified who we really are and learned enough about ourselves to live freely and positively.

Ladies, it is imperative that you identify for yourself, your likes, dislikes, wants, and desires. Knowing who you are will save you in those moments when you're trying to figure out why you act or react in a particular way.

If you are familiar with yourself and can fully identify with who you are and why you do what you do, then you will be more successful in relationships of all kinds.

Identifying certain qualities and attributes that are unique to you is also essential to your full and complete development. It keeps you from inappropriately handling or using/abusing people. For example if you are a mother or a teacher and you are used to talking to children in a "telling tone," you have to remember to switch that voice off when talking to your spouse, family, friends, and colleagues. You are a woman who is a mother but do not play the mother role all the time. Identify, acknowledge, and submit to what role or position you are in at that moment. A wife is not a mother, a daughter is not a friend, a sister is not a dictator, and a friend is not a mother. Kind of confusing? Well, imagine how the friend feels when her girl is telling her what to do and how to do it all the time. Sometimes people just need us to listen. *(See L)*

Being able to identify who you are and what is acceptable to you (what you like) will help you assume the role with humility *(see H)*, maintain your position with joy and excitement. *(See K)* and most of all, help you keep *IT* together.

GEORGE TALKS...

Who are you? No, really, who are you? Can you describe five good things about yourself? Can you identify why you act the way you do or why you get mad when certain things happen? Most people struggle with knowing themselves and their triggers. As a result of not knowing yourself, you lose the ability to control how you operate in your relationships.

Knowing yourself is the first step to building a quality romantic relationship, family system, friendship, and work environment. What usually stops people from knowing themselves is taking time for you and self-reflection. My challenge to you is to take time out for yourself, and during that time get to know who you really are so you can identify yourself when you look in the mirror.

J

JUST

in keeping with truth or fact; true; correct.

Issue: We tend to operate unfairly; using our own opinions, agendas and goals as motivating factors, subsequently being unjust.

Ladies, be fair and just in all of your dealings. Think first about the other person and the background surrounding their request or need at the time. Then consider yourself and how you are built to handle that request before you respond. We know these steps may seem like a lot, but it eventually becomes like second nature to listen, and then speak. *(See L)*

Like the blind scales of justice, we need not just see our stake in the situation but recognize that if you are involved, you somehow put yourself there. You must be blind to your desires and open your eyes to the truth of what you are saying and doing and how that is impacting all parties involved.

One example of being fair or just is knowing you are right and not having to prove it. You do not have to break someone's pride just because you can. When it is in your power to do good, do it! Find high moral ground and stand on it! Understanding that it is ok to disagree, especially when dealing with opinions *(See O)* helps to ease the desire of always having to show you are right.

Ladies, let's try being fair, not selfish or self-serving, and that should help us keep *IT* together.

GEORGE TALKS...

The word *just* has a noble, honorable, even elegant ring to it. When's the last time you felt noble, honorable, or elegant? When's the last time someone said you were noble, honorable, or elegant? Being just means doing what's right, what's appropriate for the situation. When you do what's right and appropriate, people see you as the honorable person in the neighborhood, the noble person in the family, and the elegant one in the group of friends.

Yes, it's hard sometimes to do what's right or appropriate, but in the end its best thing to do. You feel better about yourself and your decision. In addition, others will respect you for your decision and look to you for future guidance.

K

KIN · DLE

to excite; stir up or set going; animate; rouse; inflame.

Issue: Our flame has gone out and we are waiting for someone else to come by and start it. We need to learn how to excite and motivate ourselves.

Ladies!!! Kindle the fires of peace, ignite love, and jump-start compassion for your fellow man.

Let's honestly reflect on our dealings, measure our intentions, and stir up the correct emotions for the situation. Most of your interactions with people should be positive, but if you're in a situation that it isn't going well, you have the power to ignite love and understanding. *(See U)* Unconditional love is so powerful that it is more than an emotion. It is a force that if used appropriately can soothe or remedy any circumstance or situation. If ignited, like a flame, it would consume the hurt, burn away the pain, and engulf you in compassion.

Sometimes you may find it hard to be compassionate because most of the time you feel the way you were taught or trained to feel about the situation.

Let go of that and reach for the hidden truth that lies behind the why. Once you tap in, identify the areas of weakness and allow love to heal you so that compassion can be kindled.

Please know that none of these qualities come naturally. We are human and are taught, by nature, to protect and preserve at all cost. That's why it takes action on our part; you must kindle, ignite, or start up these attributes in order to keep *IT* together.

GEORGE TALKS...

Being around the right person can ignite passion in you to pursue your dreams, be a better person, and reach greater heights. What if you were that person? What if you ignited others to be greater? What if your presence kindled passion and greatness in others? That possibility is closer than you think, but it will require some adjustments on your part.

First believe the best for yourself so you can kindle the same behavior in others. Second, live your life passionately and go after your dreams. Your actions will inspire others to do the same. Last, even when you are overwhelmed and feel defeated, keep pushing towards your goal. This will further kindle others to live their life to the fullest as they see you do the same.

L

LIS · TEN

to give attention with the ear; attend closely for the purpose
of hearing; give ear; to pay attention; heed; obey.

**Issue: Most of us DO NOT listen. It is the most difficult thing for us to do,
especially when we think we are right.**

Ladies, we must admit listening isn't one of our greatest attributes. We tend to have
selective hearing that is generally used to prove a point. We hear what we want to
hear and compare it against the conclusions we've already drawn.

Because we don't listen, we must actively and consistently work on our listening
skills. Listening is a sign of respect. When we listen, we show honor and respect to
others. When we honor others, we honor ourselves. We can't listen with self-serving
intentions. We must open our ears to the hearts and minds of the people around us,
which is an ultimate sign of respect.

Women are blessed with the ability to interpret information and evaluate data,
which ultimately produces results. Unfortunately, because of our poor listening
skills, we can gather data and draw some of the best (and worst) conclusions known
to man. This can be easily avoided by becoming an active, compassionate listener.

One more reason we may be quick to speak is because we want to quickly get off
our chest, how we feel *(see E)*. Remember, it's not about what we feel; it's about what
we know. Take turns and become an active listener. Listening to the entirety of the
presentation before you draw your conclusion will help you keep *IT* together.

GEORGE TALKS...

One of Dr. Stephen Covey's principles from his famous book, Seven Habits of Highly Successful People, is seek first to understand before seeking to be understood. The premise of this principle is the importance of listening. Too often our goal is first to be understood. So, we make elaborate points, speak from our emotions, and discredit what the other person is trying to say. If we did the opposite and pushed to understand the person, we will be more successful in our interactions and in life.

Seeking to understand means we listen to others and ask questions to clarify so we get what they are trying to say. When we listen and understand others, it is easier to share our point. Sometimes we could believe the same thing, but we won't know until we listen. Listening to others can decrease the amount of confusion we experience and the amount of arguments we have with other people.

M

MAN · NERS

ways of behaving with reference to polite standards; a person's outward bearing; way of speaking to and treating others

Issue: We have forgotten what manners are and how to use them.

Let's get some. It is still polite and right in the twenty-first century to *mind your manners*. Remember, we are ladies, and ladies are not gentlemen. *(See X)* wWe are designed to carry ourselves with dignity and respect and saying excuse me, please, and thank you is still right.

It is also okay and good manners for a man to be a man and handle some things on a regular basis. You don't have to be everything to all people at all times. Share the wealth and burden by sharing the responsibility. If you use your manners when you want things done, you will get your goals accomplished in a peaceful manner. Being polite is a simple way to show yourself and others that you can keep *IT* together.

GEORGE TALKS...

Have you ever said to yourself, "It doesn't take all that," or "He or she didn't have to be so mean or rude?" I know you have thought or said this because, unfortunately, many people are rude, mean, and go too far. If we take an honest look, some of the people who are rude, mean, and go too far are us. It's become too easy to be rude, disrespectful, get an attitude all in an effort to get what we want, but at what expense?

Using our manners, being polite, and being nice can still be effective. Having and using your manners doesn't mean you are weak. Quite the contrary, it means that you won't take the easy way out and have boundaries, but you can remain respectful if they are violated. Don't take the easy way out. Be nicer, be respectful, and use your manners and you will get your way and experience a better reaction from others.

N

NAV·I·GATE

to move on, over, or through; to direct or manage.

Issue: We do not know how to navigate through how we feel; handle emotion.

Ladies, we must learn to navigate our way through how we truly feel about ourselves as individuals before we can truly look at how we handle ourselves with others.

Much like your life, navigation is a system or series of routes taken that end you up at a specific destination. Sometimes you intentionally stick to the route and land where you're supposed to land. Other times you listen to what others say despite what the navigation is telling you. And then sometimes the navigation is just off, not accurate.

Look at your internal navigation system. The status of your system can pretty much determine how you truly feel about yourself. If you are listening to and care about other people's opinions of you, despite what you know and believe about yourself, then you may get set off course. When this happens kindle up some love for yourself. Navigate or find your way to a place where you know yourself (*See I*), then you will be able to handle the feelings that come your way that affect your emotion. This will allow you to handle situations with others.

When engaging with other people you can navigate the conversation by thinking about outcomes ahead of time. Don't lie, but tell the truth in a way that people can be receptive. Sometimes we want people to know how we feel so bad that we take off into unchartered territory fueled solely on emotion. This only helps us to lose focus and not keep *IT* together.

We must navigate or direct a clear path to successful relationships. There is no perfect way, but a transparent, truthful one can lead to a path of healing. How deep you go into the waters is based on the circumstance. Every person is wired differently, but everyone has something in common with someone. Be willing to take the time, navigate through the mess, and find that common ground. Find that relatable space where you can connect with the other party—a past experience, present focus or future vision—whatever it is navigating your way through it will allow you to keep *IT* together.

GEORGE TALKS...

How do you get from where you are to where you want to be? You could just start moving and see if you get there, but that could result in spending extra money, time, and effort. The most efficient way is to get directions and navigate your course, whether that's going on a road trip or trying to reach a life goal. Even though we know this is the best way, we tell ourselves that we can figure it out. We say that about parenting, relationships, work, and other important aspects of our life. We spend more time, energy, and money trying to navigate these parts of our life on our own. Then if we do get help, we might not go to the right source.

In order to get to a desired goal, we need the map and instructions to navigate the path. Who do you go to? What books are you reading? Prepare, ask questions, read more, and use good resources so you can navigate to success in any and every area of your life.

O · PIN · ION

a personal view, attitude; a judgment or estimate of a person or thing with respect to character, merit.

Issue: We tend to express our opinions at inopportune times and with the expectation that it will effect or change the outcome.

Opinions! Yes Ladies, we all have them and are entitled to them, but does everyone have to know it?

One of the goals is for us to free ourselves from emotional turmoil and function from a place of logic and reasoning. Doing so would allow us to recognize that decisions should be made on fact, not on how we feel about the fact.

Opinions count, but they should not be the determining factor in decision making. Don't be afraid of opening your mind. Acquiring the knowledge that allows your opinions to be rooted in facts is okay. There is no decision like an informed decision.

You are your best ally! Also be careful not to draw conclusions solely based on people's experiences either, for you might just be getting their opinion based on their experience, not your facts. Trust yourself and measure your opinion based off of the other positive attributes and virtues you live by, some of which are found right here in The Ladies' Living Guide.

Keep in mind it's okay to keep your opinion to yourself. Every conversation is not an opportunity for you to try and persuade someone with your personal views or attitude. Sometimes people just want a listening ear. *(See L)* If you can't determine the nature of the conversation, ask. Ask if they want your opinion before you randomly give it. Embracing the notions of making informed decisions based on fact instead of opinion and recognizing when or when not to give your opinion would be a true sign of keeping *IT* together!

GEORGE TALKS...

There are some people who share too much. They get triggered by something and feel they need to share their thoughts. They start sharing and keep sharing, almost as if they don't realize that they have gone too far. Others have tuned them out, moved on, or completely ignored them. The problem with this person is that he or she wanted to share their opinion beyond wanting to truly be heard and be of impact.

Just because you have an opinion doesn't mean you need to share it. If you do share it, it's important to pay attention to the people you are talking to. Most people do not like an uninvited guest. Don't let your opinion be that unwanted, uninvited guest. Choose when to share and don't overshare. In doing this, you will be heard instead of being ignored

P

PA · TIENCE

an ability or willingness to suppress restlessness or annoyance when confronted with delay; quiet, steady perseverance; even-tempered care; diligence.

Issue: Patience is a virtue most of us haven't acquired; we don't practice patience!

Ladies, having patience is something we all desire and have asked for over and over again for centuries. But what are we really asking for?

The dictionary defines patience as:

1. The quality of being patient, as the bearing of provocation, annoyance, misfortune, or pain, without complaint, loss of temper, irritation, or the like.

2. An ability or willingness to suppress restlessness or annoyance when confronted with delay: to have patience with a slow learner.

3. Quiet, steady perseverance; even-tempered care; diligence

Yes the definition is written twice because I don't think we realize the depths of what it means to be patient. If we ask for patience, then many opportunities to exercise this quality will come your way.

Be careful what you wish for because you just might get it; asking for patience doesn't help. All we really have to do is understand what it truly means. Let's stop asking for patience and just be patient. Be willing to suppress restlessness, be quiet, be even-tempered, and be diligent in the situations we find ourselves in. Using every opportunity to practice patience in ourselves will result peace. Peace will then reign in all areas of your life.

Many of us feel like we are patient, but how we feel about a particular topic determines how patient we are or are not. We categorize patience according to how we feel about what we want at the time. Learn yourself. Recognize when you are being patient for some things and not for others. Let patience exist and reside in you in all things. Subsequently exercising humility (See H) and demonstrating how true Ladies use patience to keep *IT* together.

GEORGE TALKS...

Patience can be difficult because in essence it means we have to wait. Honestly, hardly anyone likes waiting. Think about the post office; it seems like there's always a line. Or the amusement park, that check that's supposed to come in the mail, or to meet someone who treats you right. We want what we want now, but when it doesn't happen in that time frame, we act out.

Patience means remaining calm or peaceful, even when you have to wait longer than you want. The benefit of being patient is that you learn more about yourself in those moments as well as keep yourself from making impulsive decisions that you have to pay for later.

QUES · TION

the act of asking or inquiring; interrogation; query.

Issue: We tend to assume instead of asking the right questions in a respectful manner.

Ladies, it is okay to question. Seeking clarity is essential to understanding. It is the nature of a woman (not necessarily a man) to want details, details, details! The more details we have, the more we "understand."

Asking the right questions at the right time is pertinent to getting the right results. We tend to nag our way to results, resulting in arguments or disagreements.

Here are a few tips to getting the results you want:

1. First, do your best to solve the problem on your own. Every issue does not deserve a question or detailed conversation.

2. Seek out the right time. Asking questions while someone is busy or participating in an activity of any kind will get you short answers.

3. Know what you are talking about. Ask one or two questions and wait for a response; don't just ramble on and on because you're emotional. Think before you speak.

4. Dialogue and discuss. Don't debate or be contentious. When you debate you are trying to persuade someone your way. Dialogue calls for mutual respect of opinions.

5. Do your best to make determinations with the variables you have and clearly identify the facts before you react.

Following these steps will help you keep *IT* together.

GEORGE TALKS...

You and I aren't mind readers. That means to get the right information or to figure out what's going on, we have to ask questions. Not only do we have to ask the question, but we have to phrase it in the way that helps us get an answer. Sometimes we focus so much on getting the answer that we rush the question. But we don't often think about the answer or the reaction ahead of time.

Think about what you want to know, think about how you would want someone to ask you, and then ask the question.

R

RE·AC·TION
action in response to some influence, event, etc.

Issue: We don't always react properly we allow our feelings to alter our emotion or state of mind.

Ladies, How many of us have ever been accused of *over*reacting? *A reaction is an action in response to some influence.* So based on its own definition, a reaction is an action prompted by a source other than yourself. True satisfaction comes when we are content and at peace with ourselves and our choices.

Stop and think about some actions you've made in response to an outside influence. How did you react? What was your retort? *Your* reactions are reserved for and belong to you. No matter what or how something is said or done; you have the right to reserve your reactions.

How do I reserve my reactions? To reserve means to keep, store, and preserve. An emotionally controlled person can and will keep their reactions by taking the time to reflect on the truth of what has transpired, adjusting to the time and space, and being patient enough to gain full understanding. *(See A, P, and U)*

Once comprehension is obtained, you must not overreact, or under react. Be aware and remember that actions beget reactions. Experience teaches that sometimes people intentionally push buttons to make you lose it, but you have got to keep *IT* together and not react based on emotion. Weigh the facts, *then* react!

GEORGE TALKS...

Reactions can occur almost instantaneously. They happen like reflexes; when the doctor hits your knee your foot kicks automatically without you doing anything. Because our reactions happen so quickly and naturally, we feel that our reactions are correct and justified.

The truth is, our reactions aren't always correct or justified. What we should aspire to get to is a response. A response means that we thought about the situation and figured out the best solution for the situation. Stop reacting all the time and start responding!

S

SAT · IS · FIED

content *or* convinced.

Issue: Are we every really satisfied? How do we know when we are?

Ladies, being satisfied is one of the things we love about life the most! We want everything to satisfy us, fit into our box, and meet our need, sometimes at any cost. True satisfaction comes when we are content and at peace with ourselves and our choices.

The first essential ingredient to satisfaction is self-satisfaction. Be content with who you are, where you are, and what you have (or do not have) at the moment.

Focusing on others keeps focus off of your own life. This is an indication that you may not be self-satisfied. Nothing in life works when your attention is on everyone else's front yard instead of your own. Use your time wisely.

Creating your environment the way you want it can lead to satisfaction. Every woman is entitled to create her environment the way she wants it, but it must be favorable for all parties involved. Your satisfaction can't be at the expense of others or determined by others. Satisfaction grows out of peace and love for mere existence. It finds joy in laughter and a song, and it rejoices in the triumphs and accomplishments of others. Being satisfied with who, what, and where you are will help you keep *IT* together.

GEORGE TALKS...

Are you satisfied? Really, are you? How do you know if you are satisfied or not? Most people think they are satisfied based on possessions and other people. What most people fail to do is base their satisfaction on themselves. Your happiness cannot be based on what someone else does or doesn't do; if that happens, you will not be happy or satisfied.

Think about you and what you need and what you have to do to get there, and then you will get closer to being satisfied.

T

TEN

a cardinal number, nine plus one.

Issue: Uncontrolled emotion gets released because we have no strategy to help control our temper.

Ladies, TEN is the new magic number. It has two benefits. First, place your feelings on a scale from 1–10. How is your emotional state being affected? 1 – Not at all to 10 – Affected to my core, I may never be the same. Doing this will help you place your feelings in perspective and also give you an opportunity to separate feelings from facts. The fact may be that even though I feel at an 8, the facts don't dictate an 8 response.

The other truth about 10 is counting to it works. Anger management counselors, exercise aficionados (enthusiast) and therapists all recommend taking a deep breath and counting to 10 in order to gain focus and relax. The problem is that in the midst of an emotional rollercoaster ride we forget to say it, sing it, shout it, count up to it, count down from it or even multiply it by 100! Most times we forget and try to fix everything in the moment. For the good of mankind, if it comes down to it, count to ten and walk away. IT IS OKAY TO WALK AWAY. Picking the conversation back up after you have had time to calm down is the best way a lady can keep *IT* together.

GEORGE TALKS…

Sometimes we take things up to level 10 when it should be level 4 or 5. Yes, you have the right to be upset, hurt, and frustrated, but everything is not a 10. Everything that happens should not bring you to 10. That probably means you are stressed and having difficulty finding other options to deal with the situation.

Sometimes, letting it go, giving the person the benefit of the doubt, or just walking away, can bring it from a 10 to a more reasonable level.

U

UN · DER · STAND · ING

mental process of a person who comprehends; knowledge of or familiarity with a particular thing; skill in dealing with or handling something.

Issue: Lack of understanding ourselves results in a lack or failure to understand others.

Understanding is a mental process that belongs to you, so therefore it begins with you.

Understanding yourself is essential to growing into the best *you* that you can be. Learn yourself. Take into consideration your life experience, and begin to comprehend why you do and say the things you do. Learn to recognize your triggers or things that cause specific reactions.

Developing a deeper connection with yourself helps open up the compassionate or empathetic side of you that tends to get shut off if we feel threatened or abused. Understanding yourself makes it easier to understand and to be understood by others.

No one should know you better than you. You can't depend on others to always give you what you want. They can only give you information that may help your understanding. To mentally comprehend what someone is saying, you must be willing and open to truly receive, thus demonstrating respect and mutual tolerance between the two parties. You must learn to become an effective and efficient communicator, intentionally and purposefully using words to convey an idea, thought, or message.

Once you show understanding, it's much easier to get it. Take time and try to understand what the others are saying. If you don't get it, ask questions *(See Q)* until you do. In everything you get in life, get understanding. Even if it hurts, it will help you keep *IT* together.

GEORGE TALKS…

How many times have you felt like someone heard what you said but based on their actions they did not understand you? Understanding is the correct application of what you heard or learned. You show others that you understand by how you act.

Are your actions showing the people around you that you understand? Understanding also requires reflecting on what you heard or learned and asking questions to clarify if anything is confusing. Have you stopped and asked any clarifying questions lately to get a better understanding? If not, do that today!

V

VOL·UME

the degree of sound intensity or audibility; loudness

Issue: When we lose control the volume tends to get higher and higher.

Dear Ladies, my sisters and my friends. Some of us have no volume buttons on our passion and desire to convey a feeling or a point. It is essential that even if we are passionate and hungry for the other person to see our point of view, we must decrease the volume so we can hear what everyone else is saying.

Controlling or monitoring and adjusting your volume levels will help you have better conversations, which will lead to more productive relationships and help you keep *IT* together.

GEORGE TALKS...

In the music world, a crescendo is used to add impact to the note and the song. In general a crescendo is used to increase the volume of a note or notes. If the volume was the same throughout the entire song, it would ruin the song, be annoying, and lose the impact. The same is the case for you. Everything and every situation should not get you to crescendo or increase your volume. Yes, there are times when it happens and when it might be necessary. But increasing your volume should happen rarely, so that when it happens someone knows this is Really, Really serious, instead of thinking that's just you being you. If being loud is your normal, you become annoying, lose your impact, and ruin how people see you.

W

WIS · DOM

the quality or state of being wise; knowledge of what is true or right coupled with just judgment as to action; insight.

Issue: By living off of our emotions, we are not using wisdom and functioning in the knowledge of what is true and right.

Ladies, *we must desire wisdom, seek to acquire it but most of all cherish it, for from it flows many wellsprings of life.*

For some reason we have adopted this notion that ignorance is bliss. Some of us, sometimes, even revert to ignorant childlike behavior; go into our girl-like voice and have "duh" moments when faced with uncomfortable situations. We act as if we don't understand for fear of exposing a weakness or flaw.

The issue we have is in not knowing. The problems arise when we embrace ignorance and keep living life as normal, not paying necessary attention to the 5 Ws. We must remember *who* we are talking to, *what* we are talking about, *where* we are, *when* we are speaking and *why* we are having this conversation in the first place.

Obtaining wisdom helps you create unified ideas and draw solid conclusions. Society in general and especially men appreciate a wise woman because she knows what to do with what she's got. Maturity comes when experience and wisdom meet. Knowing this will help you keep *IT* together.

better conversations, which will lead to more productive relationships and help you keep *IT* together.

GEORGE TALKS...

Wisdom can be acquired in many ways: from personal experiences, from a mentor, through other people's experiences, from reading/schooling, and other means. Whichever way you get it, make sure you get it. Wisdom can keep you from making mistakes and can help you get the most out of a situation. Wisdom makes you more attractive.

Would you rather be with someone who is foolish or someone who is wise? The same applies to how people see you. Wisdom can separate you from the pack, in a good way. Be unique, be better, and be wise.

X

XERX · ES

king of Persia who reigned 486–465 B.C.E., Greek Xerxes, from
O. Pers. Xayaran, lit. "male (i.e. 'hero') among kings,"
from Xaya- "king" (cf. shah) + aran "male, man."

Issue: Forsaking our feminine qualities and attributes, we tend to act like men.

Ladies, Xerxes was a Persian King who led thousands in battles across Babylon and
Egypt; his name is identified with kingship and manhood. Steve Harvey said, *"Act Like
a Lady Think Like a Man;"* he didn't say become one. You are a woman, a Queen, not
King Xerxes; *you are not a man.*

A true lady knows how to be the head of the household, the queen of the castle, the
housekeeper, and the cook simultaneously. With those many roles, why try to be the
man too? Your feminine attributes are there for a reason. We do not have to use our
power for evil, nor do we have to win every argument and conquer every city by using
your seductive words to slaughter everyone in your wake. Having the power or
knowing you are right doesn't mean you have to be right all the time.

Ladies, we do not have to dominate every decision, Allow people in your life to make
decisions for themselves. This should take a little burden off of having to control
every situation. A real lady, observes, takes notes, evaluates, and chooses her form of
reporting out; she doesn't always have to dictate and dominate. She takes in the other
twenty-five attributes found in the LLG, puts away her Xerxian desire, and proceeds
with caution. Remember you are a Lady; act like one!

GEORGE TALKS...

You should never feel like you are being controlled, fear being attacked, or be disrespected. On the other hand, men don't want to be disrespected, feel like they don't have a place/purpose, or feel like they are being controlled. In some respects the desires are similar, but how they are experienced is different.

When you act like Xerxes you can take away his place/purpose, disrespect him, and make him feel controlled. Sometimes you might act like Xerxes because you feel controlled or disrespected and feel you need to take over. The cycle is vicious and only leads to further heartache and pain. Instead of acting like Xerxes, be the queen that you are. Acting like a queen still gets you the respect you deserve and gives him the respect he deserves.

Y

YOUR · SELF

a reflexive form of you

Issue: We don't know how to JUST BE!

Ladies, it is quite all right to love yourself, learn yourself and live yourself out to be the best *you* that you can be!

There is nothing wrong with living for yourself as long as you are living. Being a lady means embracing all of whom you are—daughter, sister, wife, mother, friend, and lover. There are many facets or aspects of you wrapped up in you, but you must find and embrace the characteristics of each one.

Love yourself, learn yourself, and even laugh at yourself from time to time; this will help you keep *IT* together!!

GEORGE TALKS...

True growth comes from knowing yourself. Knowing yourself comes from self-reflection. Self- reflection comes from being able to ask yourself difficult questions, such as am I living up to my potential? What area do I need to improve? Who do I need to forgive? How can I be better than I was yesterday?

Thinking about these questions and figuring out the best answer will help you to know more about yourself. People fail to grow and be great because they fail to examine themselves and make the necessary improvements. Your success in life is linked to your ability to make the personal adjustments, especially the difficult ones, in order to be the best you that you can be.

Z

ZEAL · OUS

full of, characterized by, or due to zeal; ardently active, devoted, or diligent.

Issue: We tend to be zealous over the wrong things.

Ladies, I recommend that you go after life like a zealot!!! Take off all of your preconceived notions and live life out to the fullest. Take in a new perspective and allow this new vision to write out a different destiny, one full of successful, healthy, happy relationships.

If you are focused and zealous about your own life, then you won't be worried about others, so when the opportunity comes for engagement, you can stand and be that lady everyone will remember because she listened, she loved, and she lived life out to the fullest by keeping *IT* together!!!

GEORGE TALKS...

Have you ever seen someone who was really passionate about what they were doing? Not just happy or excited, but passionate. This person can ignite change in others and themselves. Their passion is contagious. When you are around this person you want to do more. Something about their approach, their attitude, about them makes you want to be different. It feels like they are getting the most out of their job, hobby, relationships, and life.

This person is an example. This person is zealous! Be that person. Be contagious. Be inspiring! Be zealous! Be you!

FINAL THOUGHT
KEEPING *IT* TOGETHER

Keeping *IT* Together

As you can see, keeping your *IT* together is no easy task! What does it really take to apply these twenty-six attributes to our lives? How do we achieve emotional stability and live out a life of peace?

One answer I have, proven by millions throughout the centuries, is try God. It is proven that having faith and belief that there is a greater power than you at work in your life brings peace. You no longer have to be the sole master of your fate.

You are a triune being, a person made of three parts: body, soul and spirit. Your soul is the seat or center of your emotions. Your heart and soul go together and dictate to your mind what you think. Heart and soul determine your will and your intentions. If your heart and soul are affected, everything else around you will be, too. Unfortunately, most people exist and function only in this soulish realm; forsaking the body and the spirit. This will not help you keep your *IT* together. God consciousness shifts your focus. Having a spiritual relationship provides you with wisdom and fills you with the courage to change from one emotional state to the other.

Developing spiritually helps you mature and keeps you grounded and aware of your current emotional (soul) and physical (body) states. Whatever your faith, you must seek time to grow in it. The more time you spend on the things that uplift you the less time you focus on the things that affect you.

Keeping *IT* together will always take concentrated effort. There are so many things that jar our emotional state; some things we allow, and other incidents are acts of fate. Take my word for it: once you decide to shift attention, life gets a little easier to live. Give priority to the things that matter most and recognize that emotion is a state of mind that gets altered by feelings. If you can control and maintain your Internal Transmitter then you'll have peace in your heart and mind, no matter what.

Always be encouraged! There are a range of feelings that cloud our emotional state all of the time. Our state of emotion rests upon our ability to process. Keeping your *IT* together is a choice that gets lived out over and over again every day.

Daily, sometimes hourly, we have a choice to make. Typically how we feel at the moment weighs in on the choice; therefore no important decisions or choices should be made purely out of emotion. Keeping your *IT* together allows you to weigh the options, pray for guidance, wait patiently, and choose wisely.

Maintaining your IT is a fundamental piece of the pie of life and can be established by reaching for the following goals:

• **Emotional Stability**

• **Mental Clarity**

• **Healthy prosperous relationships**

Achieving these goals can result in balance in the 5 Essential Areas of Life – *Faith, Family, Finances, Fundamentals, and Fun.*

Don't allow your IT to be taken away from you. Keep your *IT* together by balancing the 5 Areas of Life.

• **Faith** — Be firm in your faith; if you don't have any, get some. You can't achieve greatness without help from the greatest.

• **Family** — Fall in love with your family; if you don't have any, make one. Even if you don't have a biological family, find friends that you love as family, join a local fellowship (church, mosque, temple), or get married and create one, but don't live life without others to share it with.

• **Finances** — Be secure in your finances. If your credit is jacked up, fix it. There is no reason why as a lady you should not have your *IT* together financially. If you don't know what to do, there are many resources on line to help you.

• **Fundamentals** — Be rooted in essentials. Have certain standards for every area of your life. Know what you believe in. Know what you stand for. You know the old saying, "If you don't stand for something, you will fall for anything."

• **Fun** — Have fun, just do it. Life should be fun, and having it is easy. It is totally up to you to make the best out of any situation. Self-satisfaction guaranteed

Achieving balance in the five areas must be done while simultaneously seeking emotional stability. While on your journey to autonomy situations may occur or circumstances arise that test your ability to be emotionally stable.

Always remember to:

Adjust your **B**ehavior.
Control your state of mind.
Demonstrate appropriate **E**motions.
Forgive and chose Goodness while walking in **H**umility.
Identify who you truly are and live a **J**ust life.
Kindle the passion to pursue while **L**istening and minding your **M**anners.
Navigate through feelings, separate fact from **O**pinion, and practice **P**atience.
Question when you're uncertain, and reserve your
Reactions for the right time and place.
Be **S**atisfied with your choices.
Count to **T**en if overwhelmed and seek out
Understanding before you seek to be understood.
Watch your **V**olume and use **W**isdom.
You're not **X**erxes so be **Y**ourself and be **Z**ealous about life!

"Free your mind and the rest will follow!" Release yourself from emotional bondage, seek out autonomy and balance in every area of your life, and your mind will produce organized, structured thoughts that will lead you to a peaceful productive and prosperous life!

Achieve emotional maturity by keeping *IT* together!

— 30 DAY —
REFLECTION
JOURNAL

Ladies,

I encourage you to take at least 30 days to REFLECT- REPAIR- and RELEASE! Use what you have learned in the LLG to reflect on your past, repair your present and release yourself to live a well balanced, emotionally stable future.

LET'S CONTINUE THE CONVERSATION
at KarasWell.com
EDUCATE. CONNECT. TRANSFORM.

f /LADIESLIVINGGUIDE

t @LADIESLIVING

in KARA WELLS

KARASWELL

#LADIESLIVING

"ONE OF THE KEYS TO 'LADYHOOD'
IS EMOTIONAL STABILITY."

"FOSTER HEALTHY RELATIONSHIPS."

"SEPARATE FACTS FROM FEELINGS."

"ADMITTING WEAKNESS IS THE ROAD TO STRENGTH."

" COMMUNICATE EFFECTIVELY."

"CONVERT FRAGILE EMOTIONS
INTO STRONG ONES."

"TAKE TIME TO EXPLORE THE POSITIVES."

"EVERY LADY IS A WOMAN
BUT NOT EVERY WOMAN IS A LADY."

"THERE ARE MANY FEELINGS
BUT ONLY ONE EMOTION."

"ACCEPT YOURSELF."

"LOVE YOURSELF."

"A LADY IS ELEGANT AND EDUCATED, CULTURED
AND CLASSY AND DIGNIFIED AND DETERMINED."

"TAKE THE CHANCE."

"FORGIVE YOURSELF
AND OTHERS."

"CONSIDER ALL INVOLVED PARTIES,
INCLUDING YOURSELF."

"STOP REACTING
AND START RESPONDING."

"FAITH IS THE CATALYST
FOR SUCCESS."

"GIVE PRIORITY TO THE THINGS
THAT MATTER MOST."

EDUCATE. CONNECT. TRANSFORM.

"ALWAYS
BE ENCOURAGED."

"SEEK OUT AUTONOMY AND BALANCE
IN EVERY AREA OF YOUR LIFE."

"KEEP YOUR IT TOGETHER."

ABOUT THE AUTHORS

KARA Y. WELLS

Kara Wells is a consummate educator, life coach and community strategist. Born and raised in New England, her transformative professional and personal journey has seen her emerge to become a poignant voice on self improvement, relationships, strategic networking and community development. Her extensive work in Boston directing community resources towards multi-dimensional early childhood education initiatives in the inner city, as well as research and development programs linking faith and family to personal and professional development gives her unique insight into the subject matter of her debut publication. Kara Wells is founder and current chief strategic navigator at KARASWELL.COM – a nexus point for self development, the dynamic exchange of ideas and professional networking within communities.

KARASWELL.COM

f /LADIESLIVINGGUIDE
t @LADIESLIVING
in KARA WELLS
KARASWELL
LADIESLIVING

GEORGE JAMES LMFT

George James is a licensed marriage and family therapist who specializes in helping couples improve the quality of their relationship, reconcile conflicts and overcome intense situations such as affairs, lack of communication, parenting struggles and much more. He also works extensively with professional athletes, adult men and young adult men on various issues including defining manhood, career and work-life balance. His expertise also includes treating actors, entertainers, college students, faith based concerns, anxiety and depression. In addition, he speaks and consults with universities, for profit & non-profit organizations and family owned businesses. Mr. James is devoted to helping people improve their quality of life, to be involved in the healing of their wounds and enrichment of their relationships. He is married to his wonderful wife, Candace and they are parents to their beautiful daughter Nalani and their cheerful son, Alexander.

GEORGETALKS.COM

🅣 @GEORGETALKSLLC
▶ GEORGETALKSLLC

Works Cited

1. Covey, Stephen. The 7 Habits of Highly Effective People. London: Simon & Schuster, 1999. Print.

2. Dictionary.com. Dictionary.com, n.d. Web. 05 Nov. 2013.

3. "Emotions." Bee Gees. Time Music International, 1997. CD.

   "Emotion" (Samantha Sang song), a song by the Bee Gees, originally recorded by Samantha Sang and covered by Destiny's Child Emotion (Barbra Streisand album), 1984 Emotion (Martina McBride album), 1999 Emotions (Brenda Lee album), 1961 "Emotions", a 1961 single by Brenda Lee Emotions (Mariah Carey album), 1991

4. Hooke, S. H. "Matthew 12:34." The Bible in Basic English. Cambridge: Cambridge UP, 1982. N. pag. Print. New King James Version

5. Morris, William. "Definition of Lady." The American Heritage Dictionary. Boston: Houghton Mifflin, 1982. N. pag. Print.

6. Webster, Noah. "Definition of Woman." New Collegiate Dictionary. A Merriam-Webster. Springfield, MA: G. & C. Merriam, 1953. N. pag. Print.

www.ingramcontent.com/pod-product-compliance
Lightning Source LLC
LaVergne TN
LVHW051246080426
835513LV00016B/1775